PSYCHOSIS

The Way In. The Way Out.

Simon Robinson

PSYCHOSIS: THE WAY IN. THE WAY OUT.

This edition is a substantially revised and expanded work,
distinct in structure, content, and presentation from earlier editions
previously published under the same title.

Revised edition published 2025

ISBN (Paperback): 978-1-918532-00-5

Simon Robinson
www.drsimonrobinson.com

Printed and distributed by IngramSpark
Printed in Australia, UK and USA

READER NOTICE:

This book reflects personal experience and interpretation.
It is not medical advice and does not replace professional care.

If you are feeling unsafe, overwhelmed, or at risk of harming yourself, please seek immediate support from a healthcare professional or a trusted local crisis service.

This book does not ask you to move faster than you can.

Nothing here requires agreement, belief, or endurance.

If at any point the material feels like too much,

stopping is part of the work.

Chapter 1

I remember the first moment the word sane stopped feeling solid.

It did not collapse.

It loosened—just enough to notice that I had been leaning on it without knowing why.

PSYCHOSIS

It felt as though a file had been opened somewhere.

Nothing was written in it.

Nothing was closed.

Thoughts began speaking to themselves.

Not arguing.

Just continuing.

Words arrived before understanding.

I learned the sounds first.

Meaning followed later, unevenly.

One side of me grew louder.

The other did not disappear.

It simply waited.

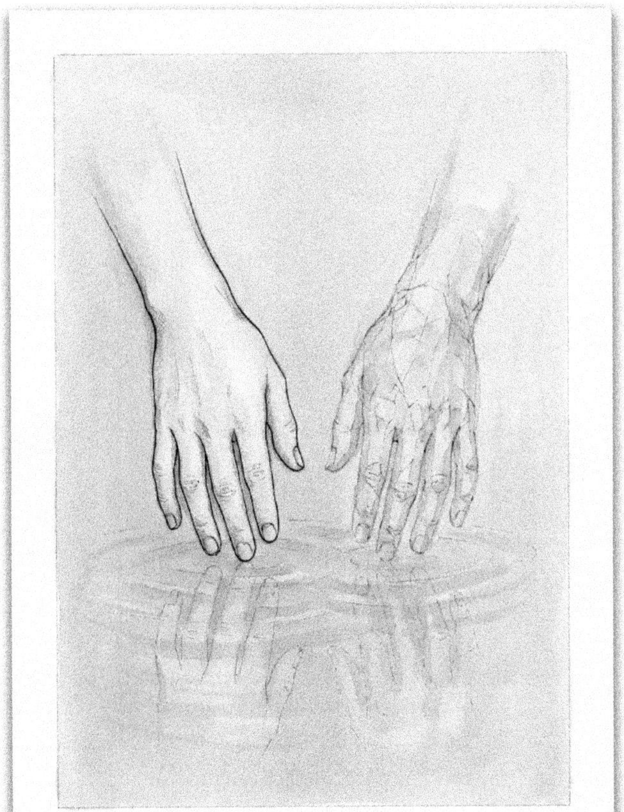

There was someone else once.

Not separate.

Just nearby.

Play stopped without explanation.

Nothing replaced it.

One voice began speaking for everything.

It was decisive.

It was alone.

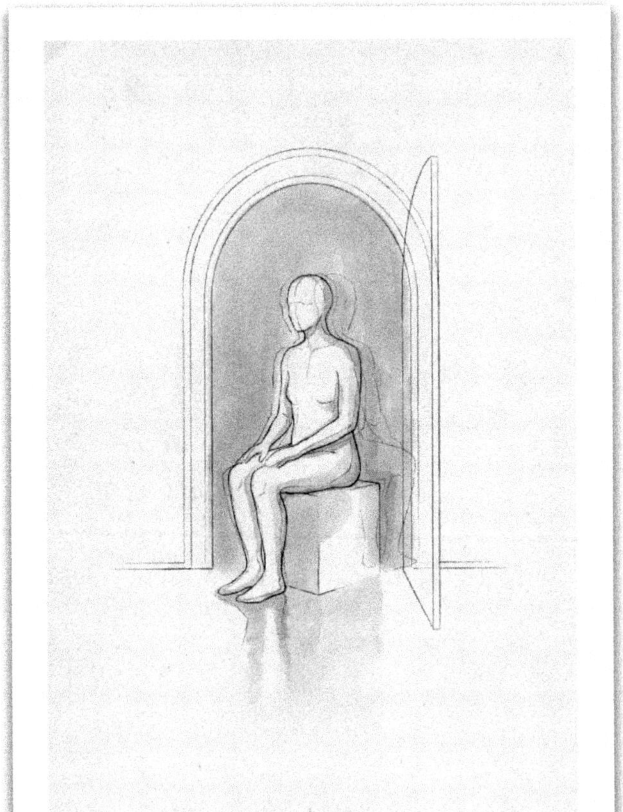

Feeling became inefficient.

Usefulness took its place.

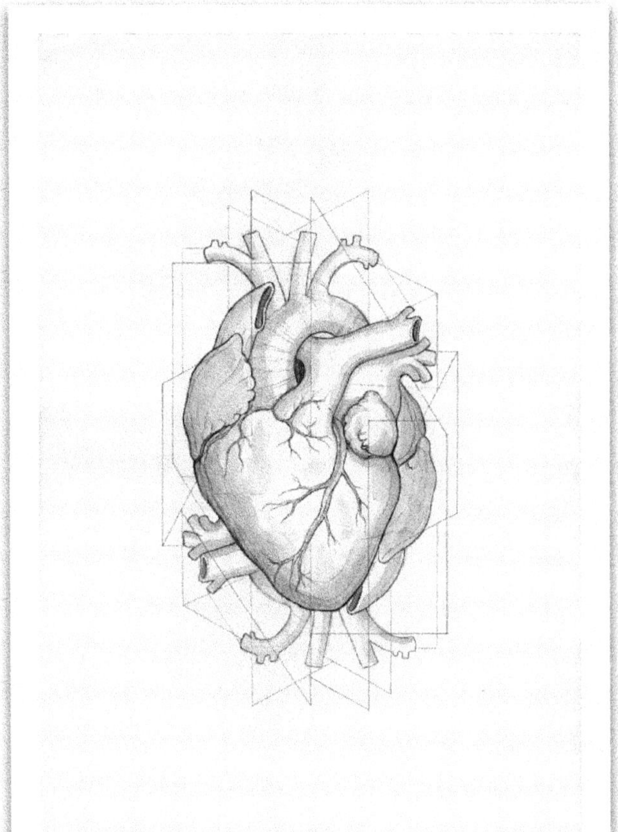

Something remained.

Unheard, but present.

Silence felt safer than explanation.

I learned to keep certain things unspoken.

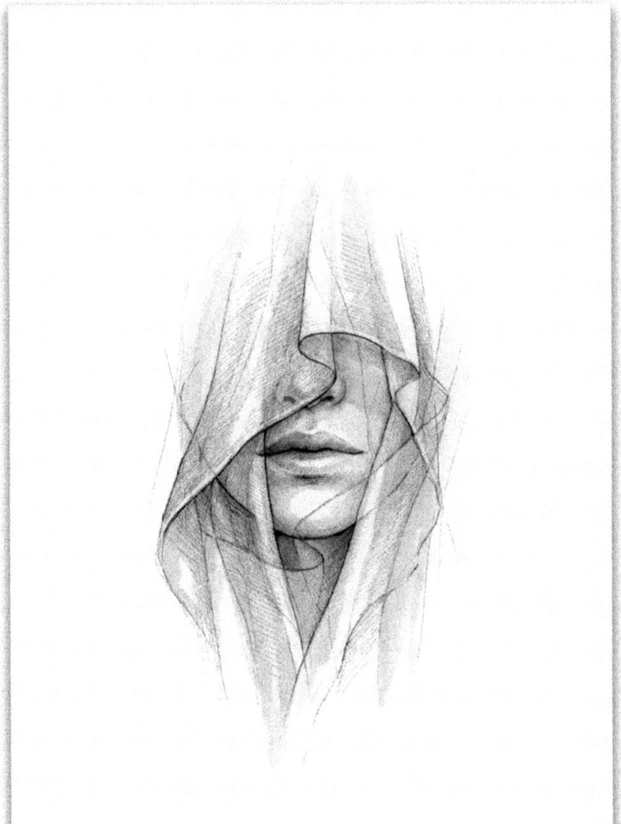

The question never closed.

It simply stayed with me.

Chapter 2

The word reality looked firm on the page.

When I said it quietly to myself, it thinned.

Nothing dramatic—just enough to notice space where there hadn't been any before.

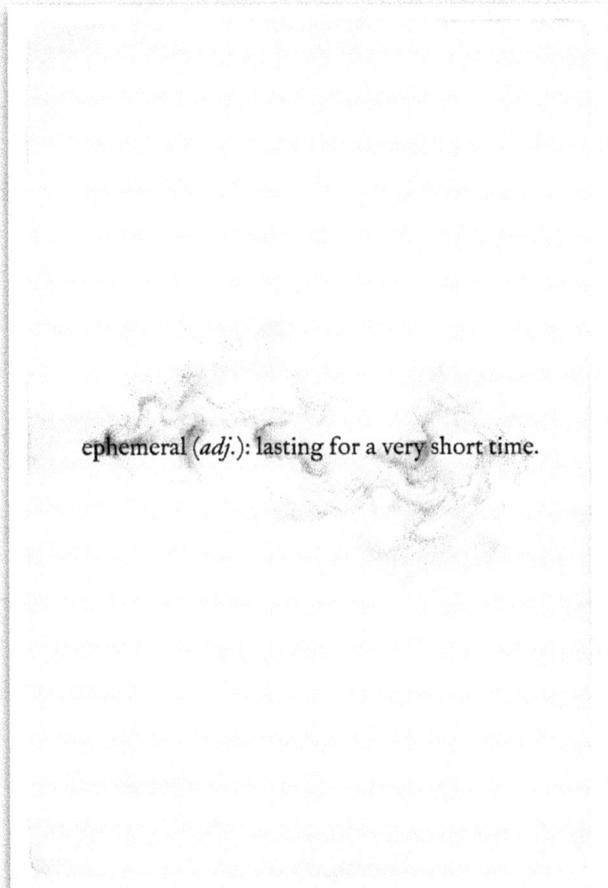
ephemeral (*adj.*): lasting for a very short time.

I remember a time when nothing needed sorting.

Play and world were not separate.

Everything that happened counted.

It wasn't panic.

More like the floor tilting a degree—

enough to feel balance shift, not enough to fall.

Something began moving without asking me.

Momentum arrived already in motion.

I noticed after the fact.

What was lost didn't announce itself.

It simply didn't return.

The grip of I loosened.

Decisions floated longer before landing.

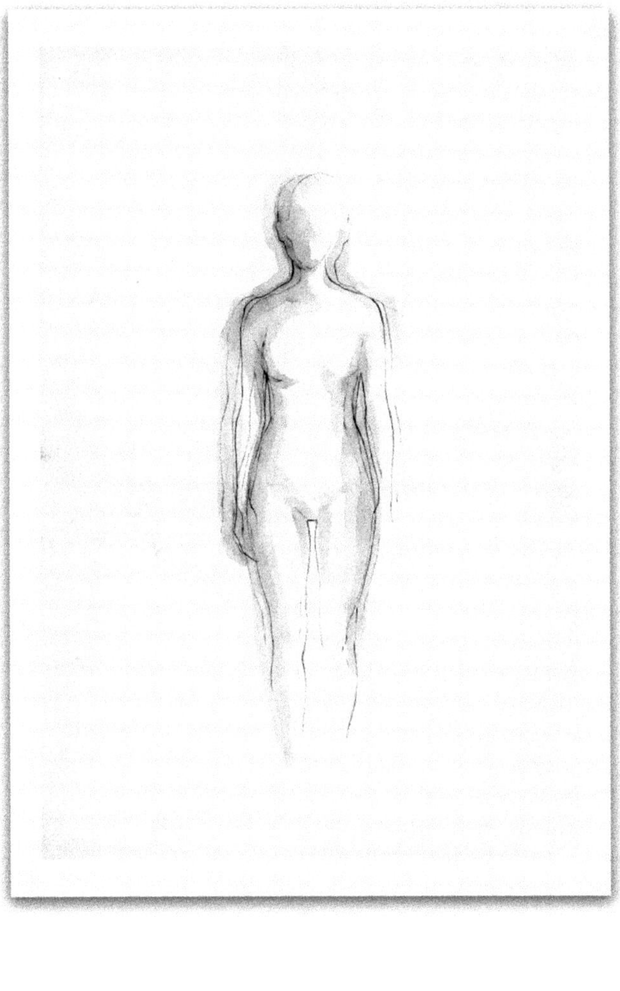

Each thought checked itself.

Then checked again.

Nothing settled for long.

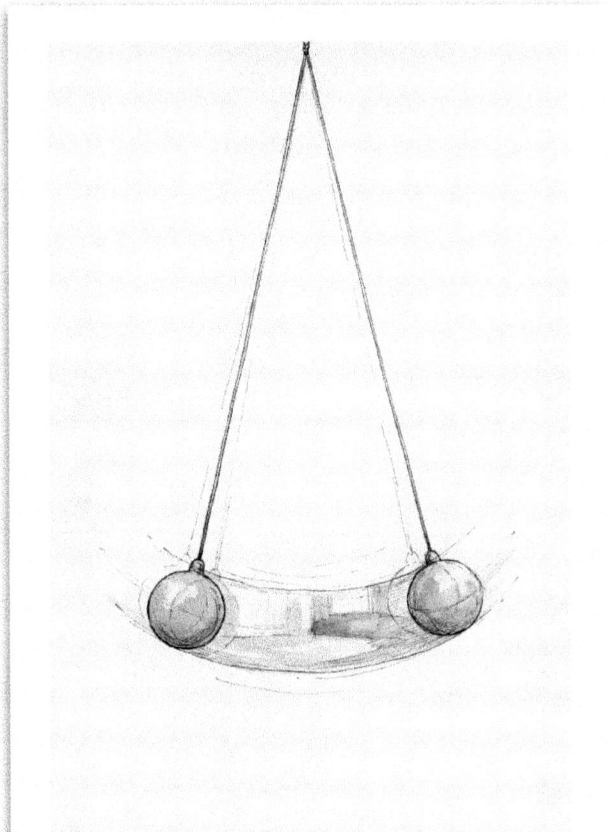

When someone else was sure,

my own experience shrank.

Not erased—just quieter.

There seemed to be more than one channel.

Not voices—just parallel noticing.

Sometimes they crossed.

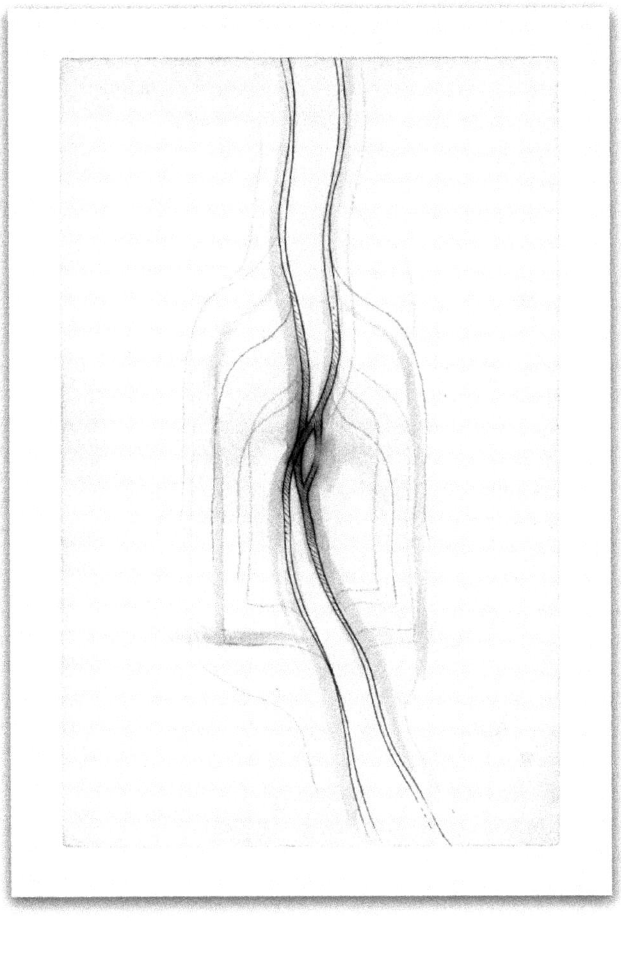

For a moment, the self softened.

The easing was real.

So was the disorientation that followed.

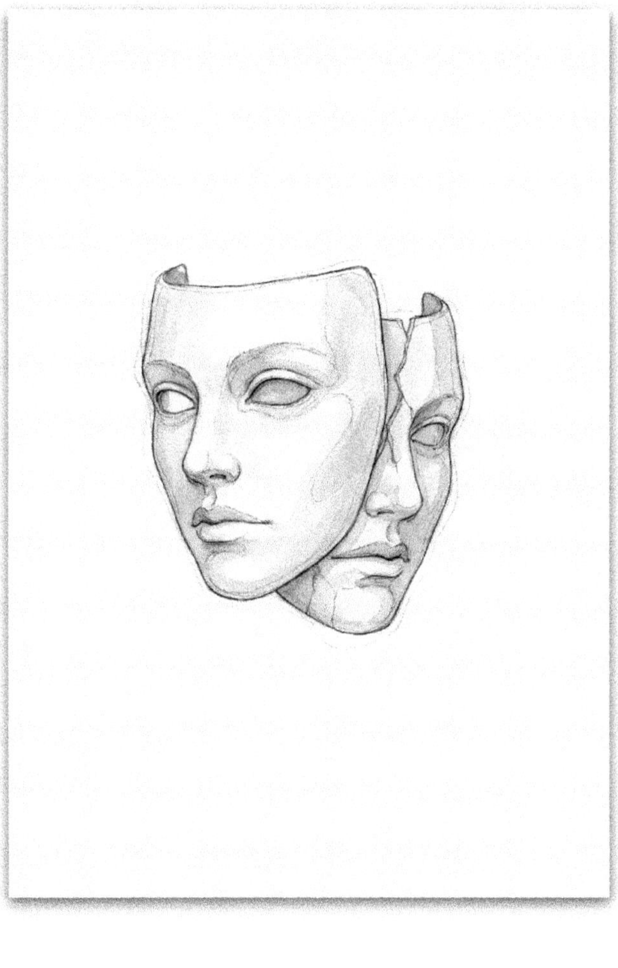

I felt placed at a distance.

Close enough to see,

far enough not to enter.

I stopped deciding what it meant.

I kept going anyway.

Chapter 3

I remember a kind of belonging that didn't need to be argued for. Not happiness exactly—more like being part of things without having to decide it.

As if the world and I were still touching at the edges, before "me" became a hard outline.

My name is a sound that points in my direction. It doesn't capture what it points to.

Sometimes it feels like a tag tied to empty air—useful for others, and only partly accurate for me.

When I hear it, I answer, but something in me arrives a fraction late.

Over time, the world kept adding notes to me. Capable.

Difficult. Quiet. Too much. Not enough.

I learned to carry these words as if they were facts, even when they contradicted each other.

It started to feel like I was made of assessments—checkboxes where a person should have been.

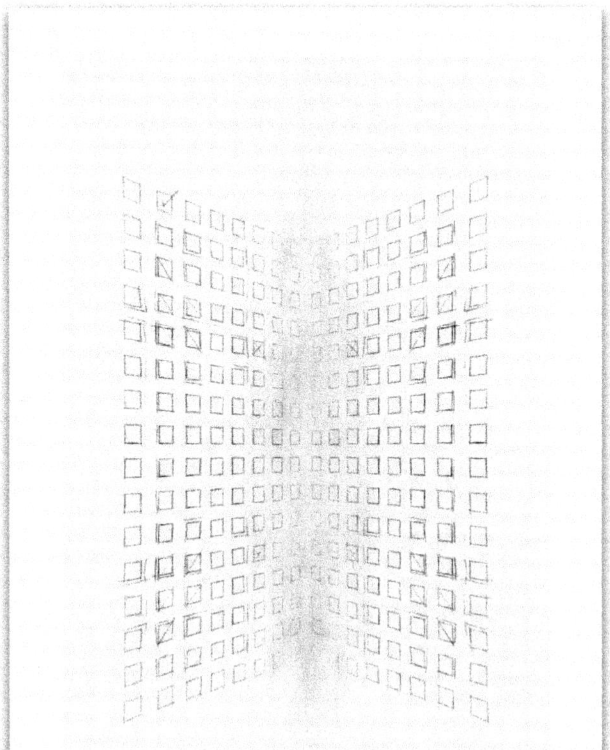

There are moments when the container shows itself. Beliefs, preferences, roles—things that usually feel like "me"—shift, and what they were holding becomes hard to find. It isn't a grand revelation. It's closer to opening a bag and meeting only air.

Sometimes the "thing" called self seems to appear only when it is named.

Parts are present—memory, sensation, habit, intention—and then, as if by a reflex, the mind draws a boundary and says: this is one.

The unity feels real enough to function. It doesn't always feel real enough to trust.

When the parts get loud, the whole becomes a suggestion.

I look at one thing and it keeps separating—detail after detail, edge after edge—until the object feels less like an object and more like a swarm of components.

It is tiring to keep recomposing a world that won't stay together.

Neutrality becomes hard to locate.

Small patterns start to glow with relevance—not with light, but with pressure—as if ordinary details are trying to speak.

I don't know if they are messages. I only know the feeling of being addressed.

I try to explain what it is like, and the words come out rigid. Inside, experience is fluid and crowded; outside, language arrives as straight lines and fixed categories. I can feel the gap—what I mean versus what can be said—and it leaves me sounding certain when I am not.

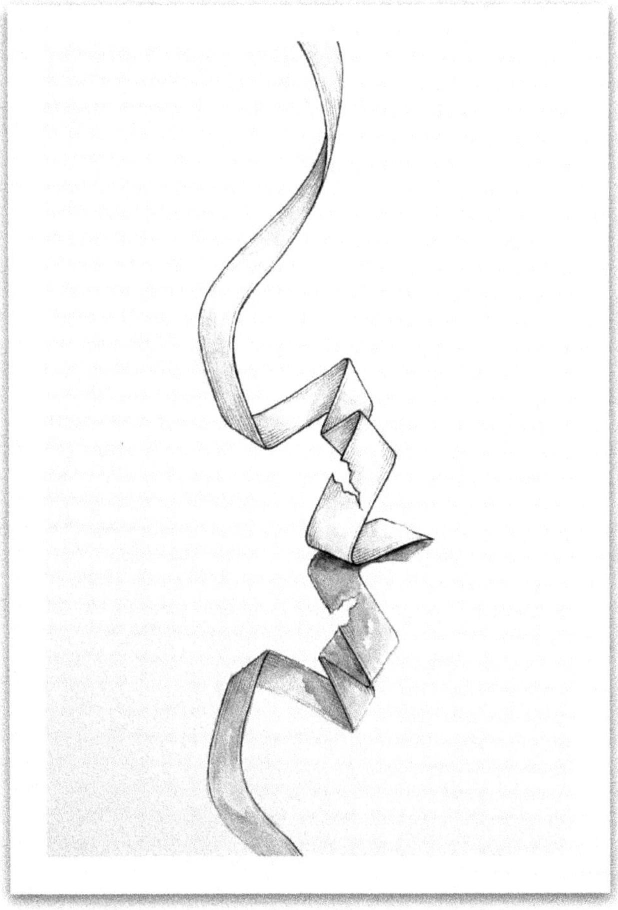

Time stops behaving like a line.

Minutes vanish. Hours thicken. I arrive late without choosing to. I start something and realise I have been elsewhere—inside thought, inside images, inside a thin dream.

It isn't always frightening. It is often just disorienting, like walking with a slight tilt.

Sometimes the page flips in my mind.

Letters feel reversible for a moment, as if direction is a choice I have to re-make. I can still read, but it takes effort—an extra step that wasn't there before.

Certainty becomes a small manual task.

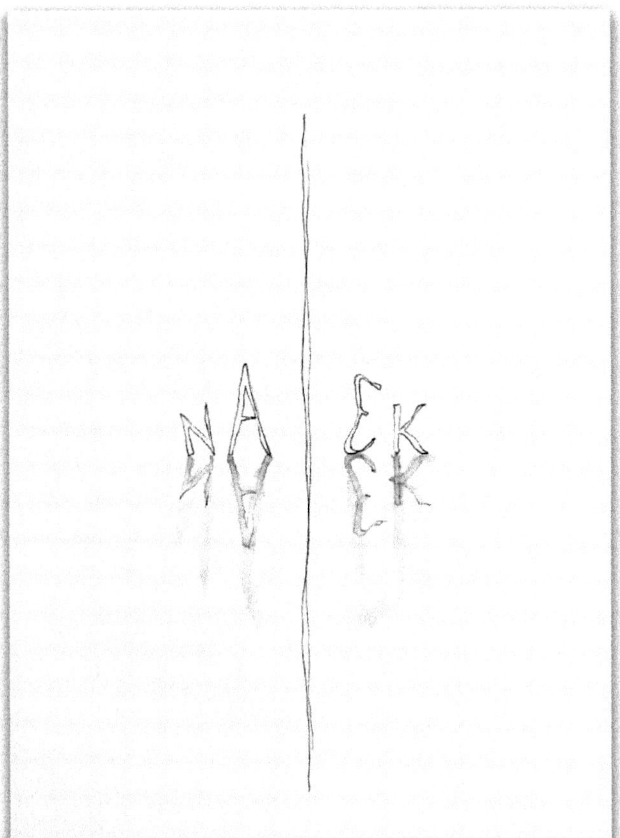
NA ЄK

There is a sense of being too close to the workings.

Things that used to run quietly in the background become audible: the sorting, the scanning, the constant checking for what something means.

It can feel like living in a room where the walls are thin and every pipe can be heard.

I can sense the next door.

Not a dramatic gate—just a shift in tone, a nearer darkness, a place I don't want to invent stories about. I don't rush it.

I hold the tension as carefully as I can: enough honesty to stay present, enough restraint not to turn it into a verdict.

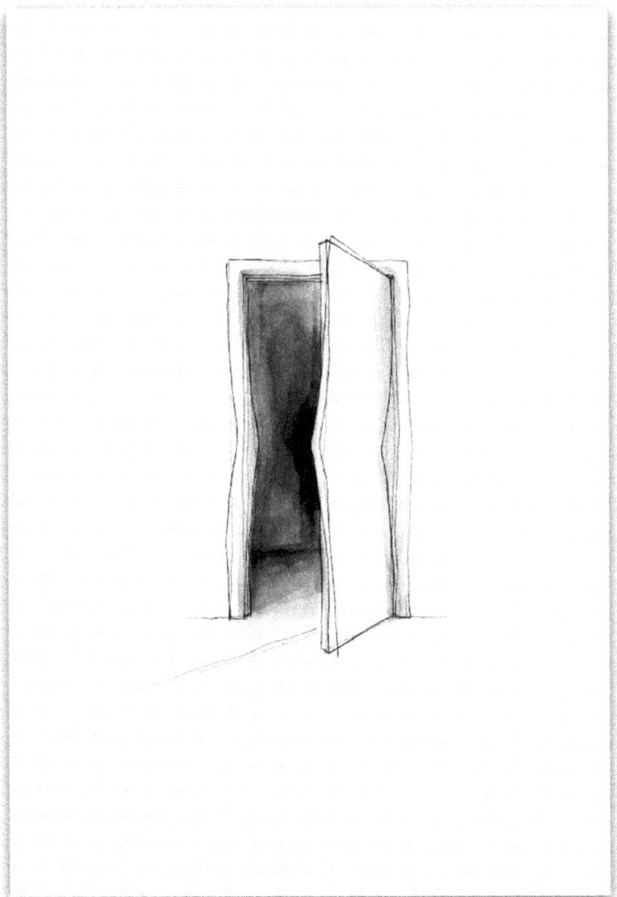

Chapter 4

I start from a place that feels unheld.

Not dramatic—just thin.

I step forward without a solid "me" to carry.

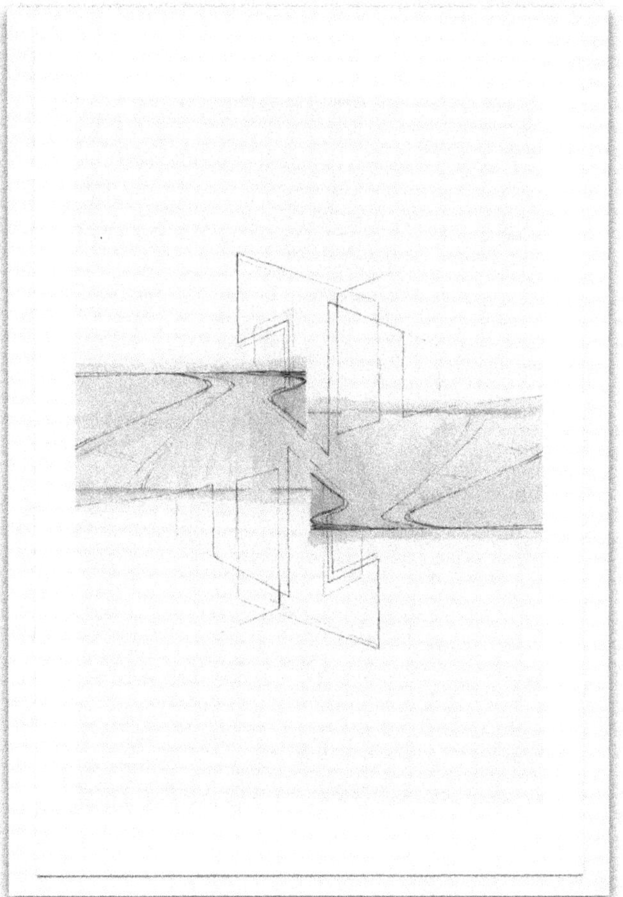

I feel pulled between currents.

One drags downward into bluntness.

One lifts toward tenderness I can't quite trust.

Something old stirs low in the body.

Wordless, close, and difficult to locate.

It feels like a knot below speech.

I sense earlier versions of myself still present.

Not as memories, exactly—more like residues that never fully emptied out.

I meet them as atmosphere.

I sense earlier versions of myself still present.

Not as memories, exactly—more like residues that never fully emptied out.

I meet them as atmosphere.

Parts of me appear like strangers in my own house.

They don't introduce themselves.

They simply stand there—distinct, unmerged.

At the edge of attention, there is gathering.

Not words I can quote—more like a pull toward

chatter and suspicion.

Soft, persistent, almost polite.

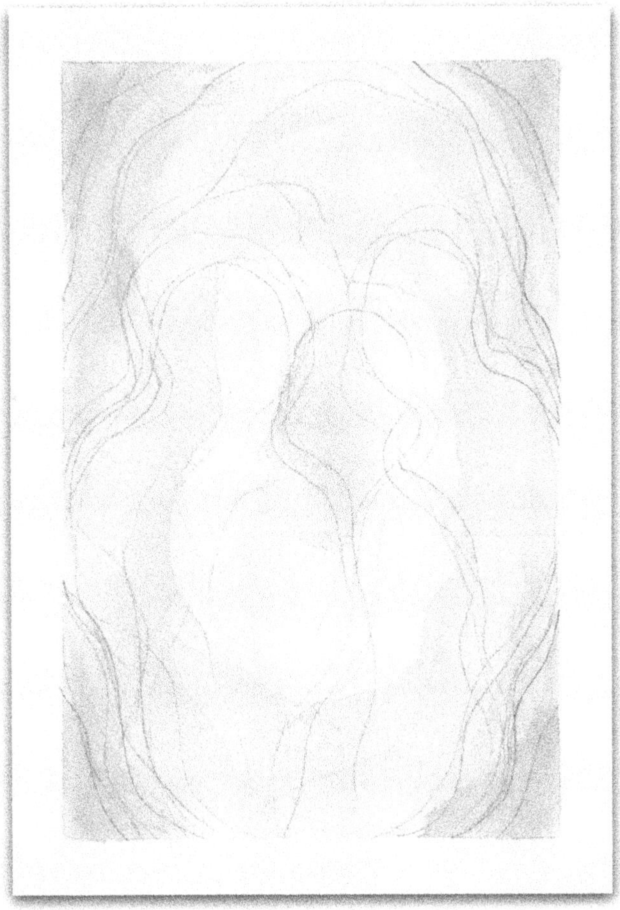

Perception begins to stain.

The same world is there, but it looks slightly poisoned—

as if seen through residue.

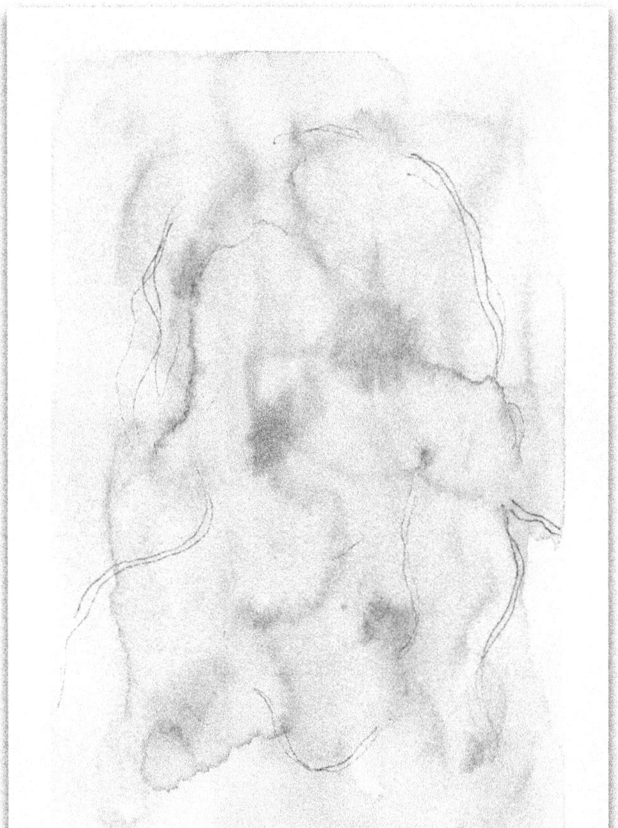

A hard inner voice demands certainty.

It speaks in absolutes in a place that won't hold them.

The pressure is the point.

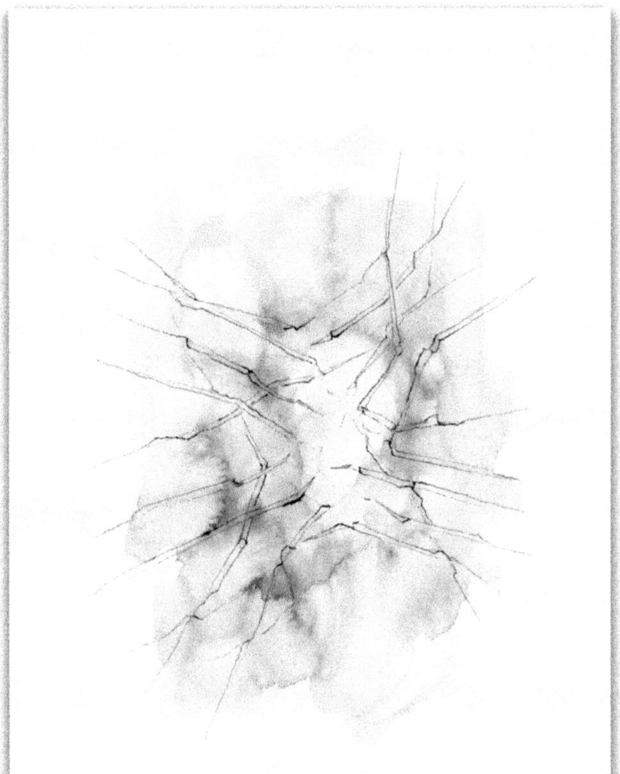

Heat gathers.

The mind imagines repayment.

It feels self-justifying, and that frightens me more than the anger itself.

Everything turns sour and distant.

Joy feels like it belongs to someone else.

I watch life through a dull pane.

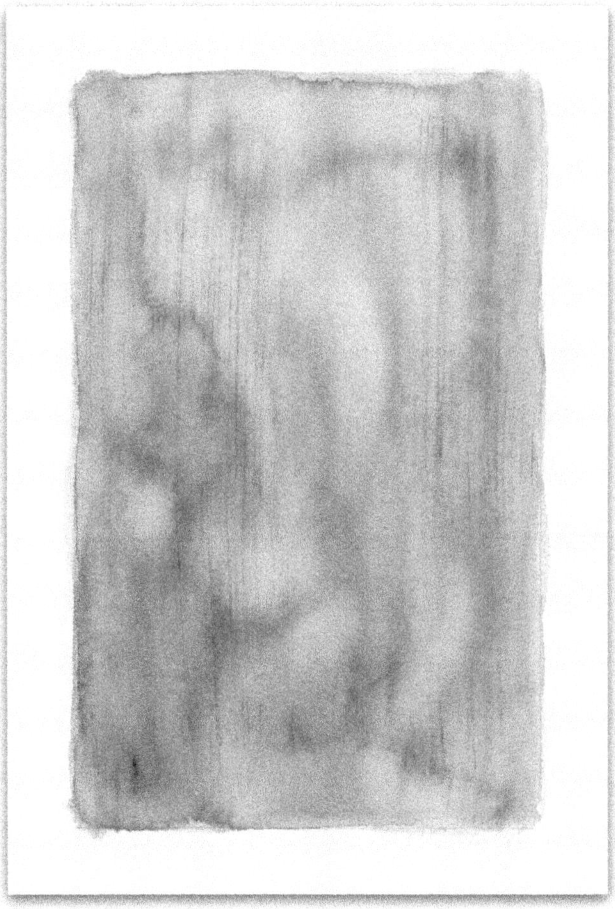

There is a stretch where meaning drops away.

Not insight—just absence.

The dark feels vast and impersonal.

Scenes shift without explanation.

Logic doesn't govern; it only arrives late, trying to catch up.

Characters won't stay consistent long enough to trust.

I feel a deep separation—inside and outside becoming two.

Not a story, not a theory.

Just the sensation of a cut.

Words feel like wind.

When I name something, it sharpens.

Silence feels safer—not as a solution,

but as a way not to feed it.

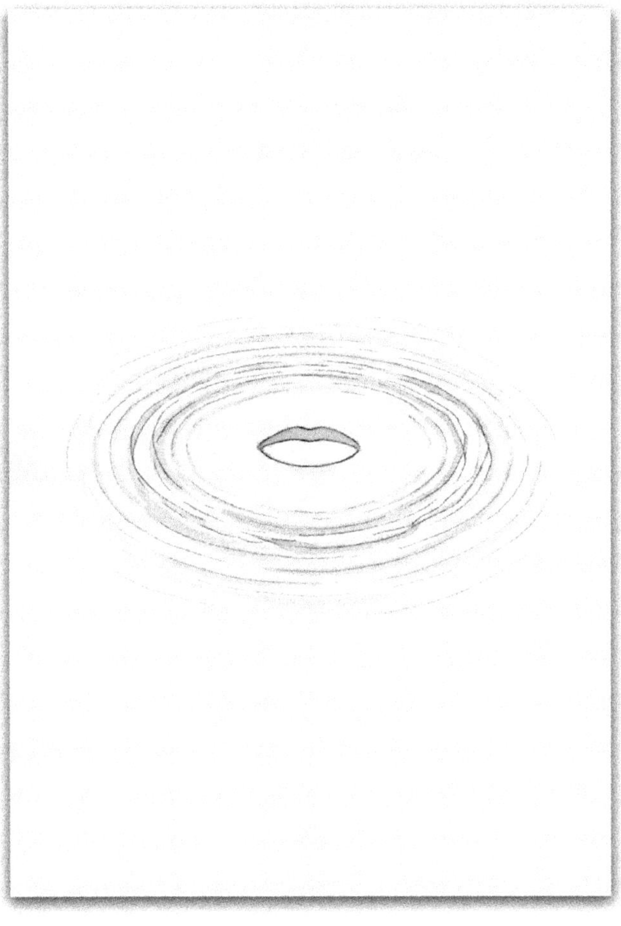

Chapter 5

"In the beginning was the Word..." — Gospel of John 1:1.

I had heard it before, as cadence.

This time it landed with weight, like a bell struck once and left ringing.

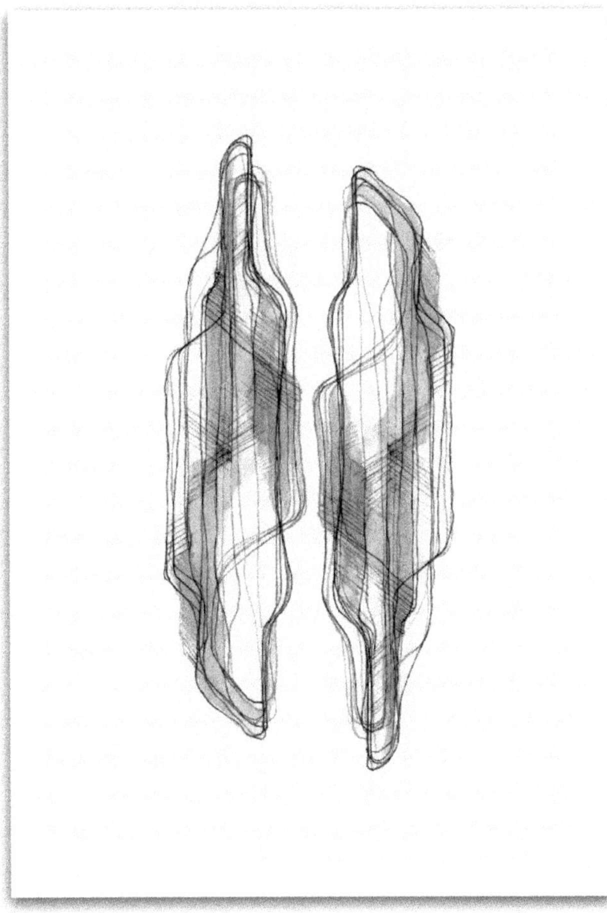

The shapes of letters began to feel older than the mouth that spoke them.

As if the alphabet was not just a tool, but a buried structure I had been walking on without noticing.

Experience still happens without naming.

But words give it edges.

Without labels, it feels wider—and harder to hold.

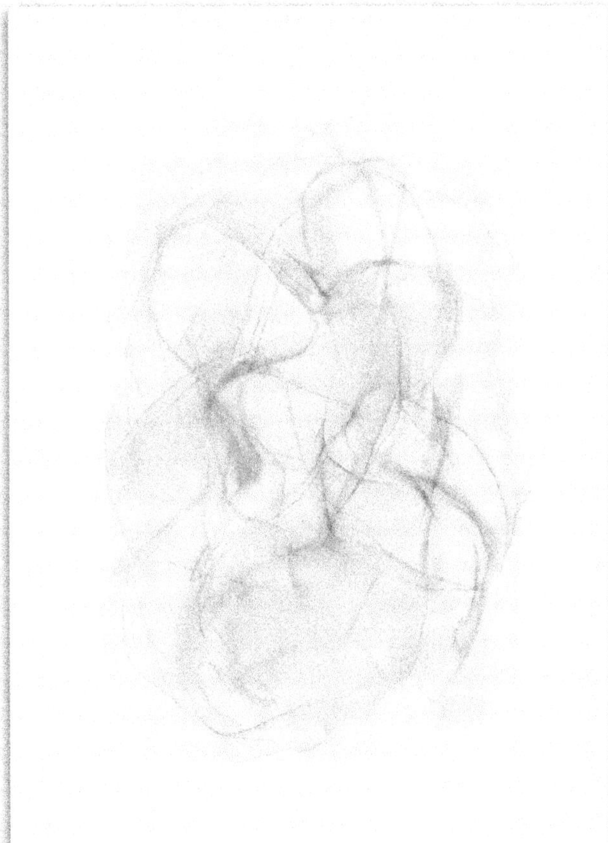

Precision increases.

Something wider goes quiet.

The chosen channel becomes efficient, and the rest becomes background.

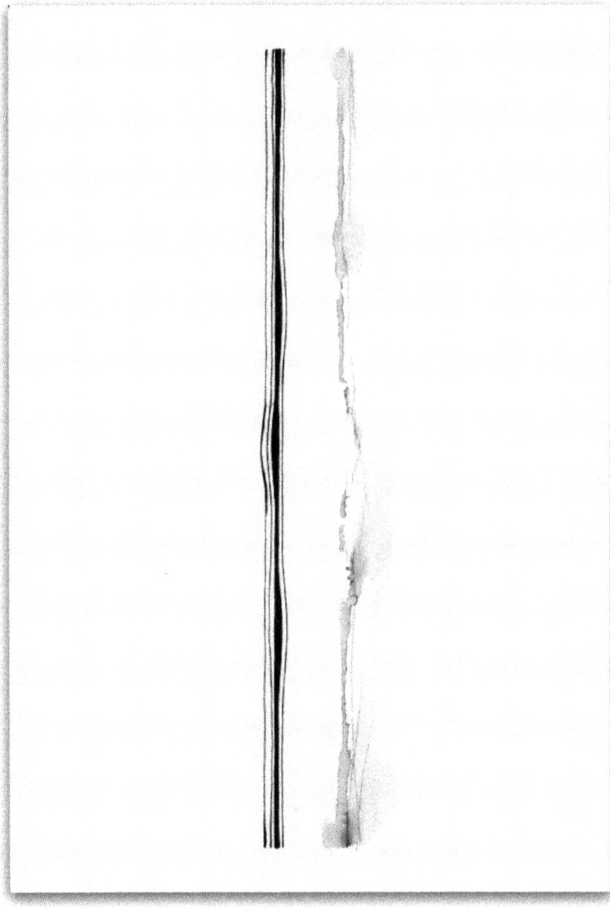

I notice a second track of awareness.

Not a voice, not a message—just an extra angle.

I keep it hidden, even from myself.

Something long-dormant opens again.

Too fast to explain.

Bright enough to make me cautious.

I try to force coherence onto what won't hold it.

The effort becomes visible as strain—

like tightening a net over smoke.

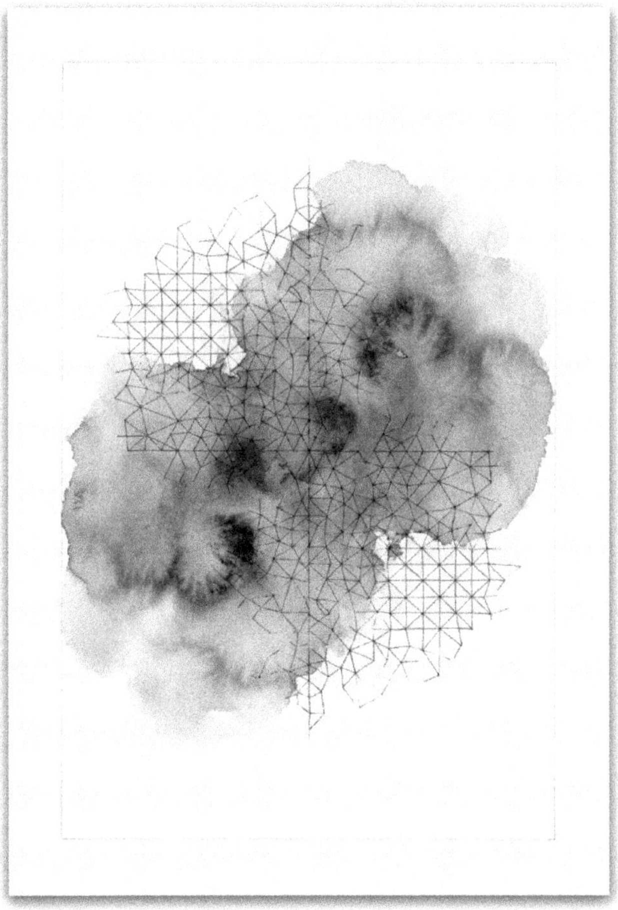

Amid shifting thought, something remains.

Not a conclusion—just a steadiness that doesn't argue.

It feels impersonal, and it stays.

I point at what can't be named.

I call it it, because language demands something to hold.

Then the pointer becomes the story.

Half-truths start to sound louder than they used to.

Evasion becomes visible in the gaps.

I don't confront it. I just notice how it lands in me.

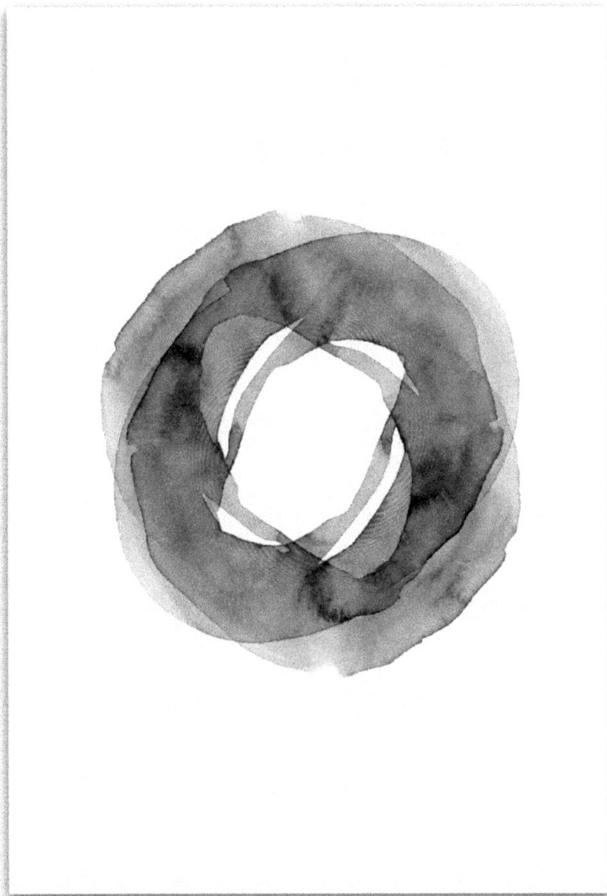

I choose not to speak.

It feels safer.

It also feels lonelier.

Old reasons dissolve.

Days stretch without shape.

I watch time pass as if it belongs to someone else.

The small maintenance of being human becomes strangely hard.

Hygiene. Food. Teeth. Clothing.

Nothing tragic—just an ordinary unraveling I don't know how to explain.

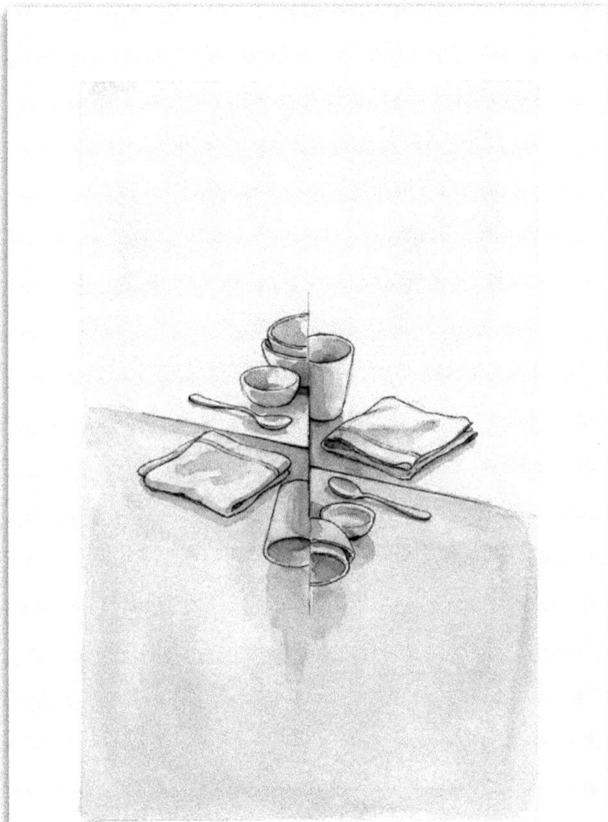

In public I feel cut off.

In private I feel accompanied—

not by answers, only by presence.

Chapter 6

I saw the word metamorphosis in plain print—almost clinical.

For a moment it didn't read like biology.

It read like my life, written from the outside.

I used to believe adulthood meant being set.

Now the "fixed" feeling looks brittle—

a hard shell that can crack without warning.

Even here, something remains quiet.

It watches without speaking.

Not comfort—just steadiness that doesn't take sides.

Thoughts pass through like weather.

Some are sharp. Some are dull.

None of them fully qualify as me.

Certain sentences leave a mark when repeated.

Not magic—just how a phrase can press into mood and body.

I notice the bruise-like residue after saying it too many times.

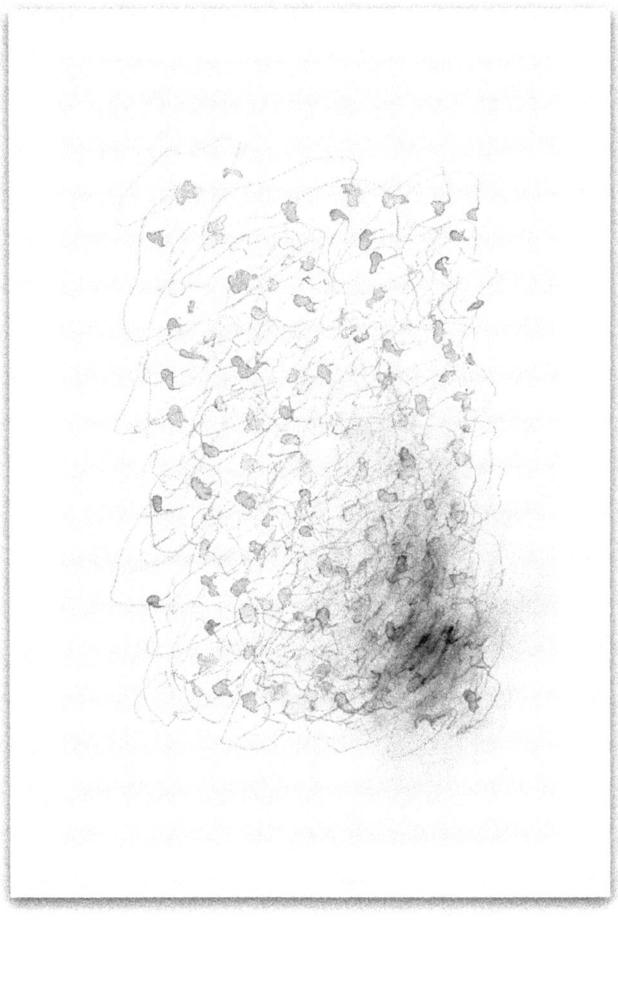

When something inside feels boundless,

a name can give it an edge.

Not a cure—just a boundary.

Without that, it spreads into everything.

There is a kind of inner agitation that senses fear.

The more distressed I am, the more it stirs.

When I stop bracing, it sometimes settles on its own.

I try to explain, and watch people fail to follow.

The gap lands as heat in the chest—

not anger, more like futility.

I learn to wear normality like a clean shirt.

It helps me move through the day without being questioned.

Inside, the weather keeps changing anyway.

A feeling arrives in me with no clear origin.

It could be mine. It could be borrowed.

The uncertainty is what makes it confusing.

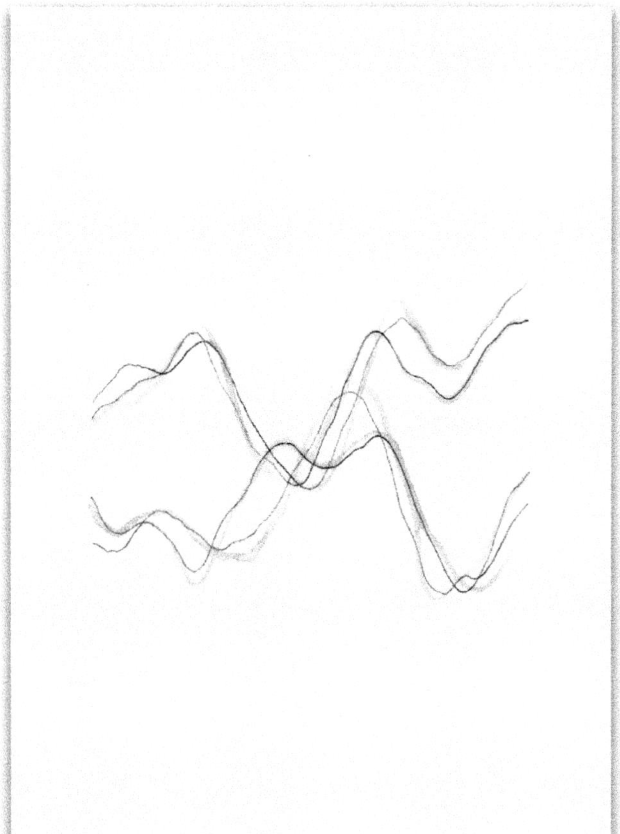

I react to a tension I can't prove.

The reaction becomes the evidence, and the room tightens.

Afterward, I'm left with the same question: what did I actually hear?

The day needs rails.

Without structure, it spills everywhere—

thought, sensation, time, all of it.

I choose what I can carry.

Small tasks. Short distances.

The rest waits, whether I like it or not.

I keep it close.

I watch the urge to perform it—to turn it into certainty.

Speech can inflate things that shrink in silence.

Chapter 7

I realise I am halfway through something.

Not in a celebratory way—more like noticing a marker by the road.

The relief comes quietly, without promise.

What I was told does not quite match what I am in.

Two versions of the world overlap,

but they do not settle into one.

The gap between them carries a low, constant tension.

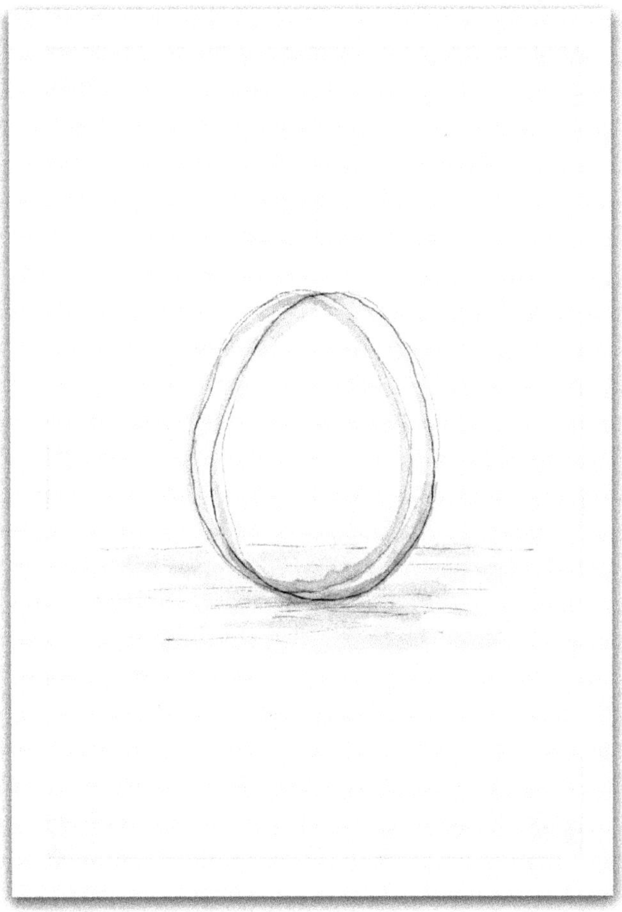

After the worst effort burns out, something quieter remains.

Not peace exactly—more an absence of struggle.

The air feels emptied rather than resolved.

A sharp idea flashes—how easily I could shock or unsettle.

It has energy, but it feels borrowed.

I recognise it as movement away from centre, not toward it.

Even alone, I feel the weight of being answerable.

Family, history, and outcome stand quietly nearby.

Nothing needs to be said for consequence to be present.

I start borrowing words that feel provisional.

They gesture toward something I keep encountering,

without proving it.

The vocabulary arrives after the experience, not before.

Things feel nearer than they should.

As if the world is not only present, but directed.

The feeling unsettles more than it persuades.

An object holds weight far beyond its shape.

The meaning is not in it, yet it stays with it.

Touch alone seems enough to activate memory.

In dreams, everyone arrives at once.

The dead, the past, the impossible—none ask permission.

Time loosens without explanation.

A knowing lands fully formed.

Explanations trail behind it, if they come at all.

I note the order carefully.

Patterns gather without effort.

They repeat just enough to feel intentional.

I resist naming an arranger.

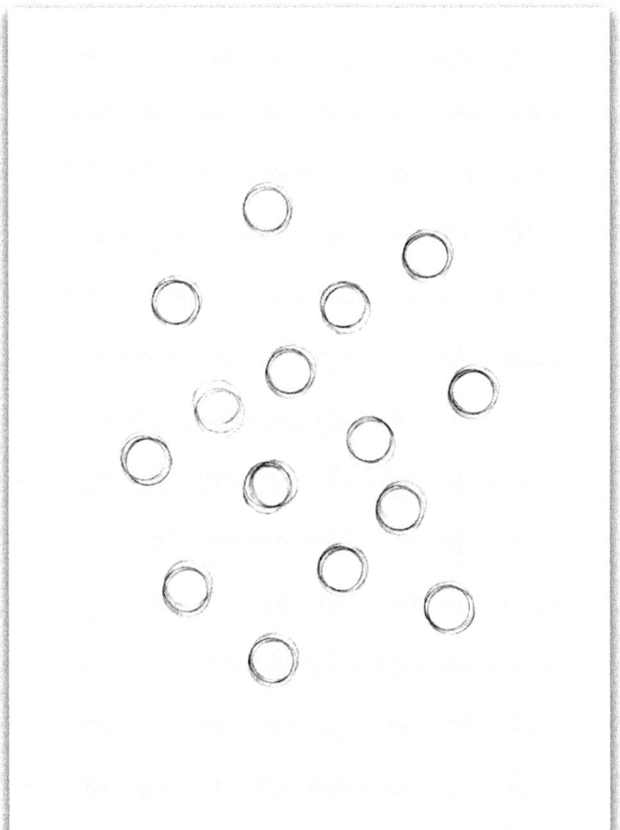

The experience flatters me.

For a moment, it places me at the centre.

I feel the cost embedded in the offer.

I learn to hold what I notice inwardly.

Speaking less becomes a form of care.

The silence carries its own tension.

I keep moving, without conclusion.

Curiosity stays, but it does not lead.

Nothing is taken as proof.

Chapter 8

Something shifts.

What used to arrive as weather now arrives with names.

The field feels indexed, as if I could file what I'm noticing—

—and the filing itself feels consequential.

I start holding the world vertically.
Not higher and lower in any heroic sense—
just levels that seem to press against each other,
like thin sheets you can't quite separate.

I watch structures appear before I can justify them.

Lines, scaffolds, corridors—drawn in the mind first,

then haunting the room like a draft overlay.

I can't tell which part is "mine," only that it arrives.

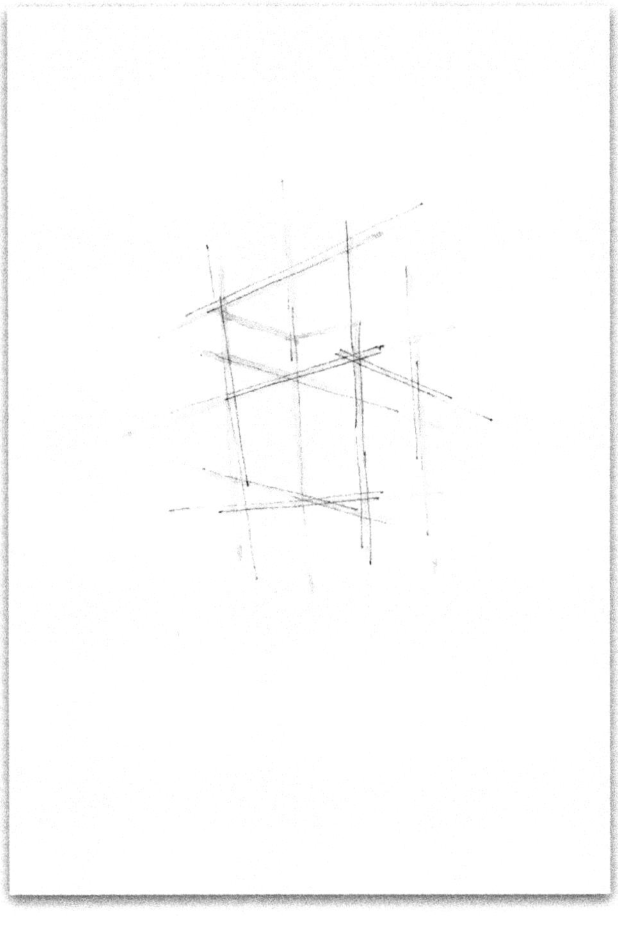

When I name a thing, it sharpens.

A loose shape seems to tighten into a "something."

That tightening feels powerful—

and slightly unsafe.

Inside the dream-quality of things,

another awareness flickers on.

It watches without interrupting.

Not an answer—

just a second register running alongside.

Where there used to be only space, I sense presences.

Not clear beings—more like impressions that take up room.

The ordinary world feels quietly crowded at the edges.

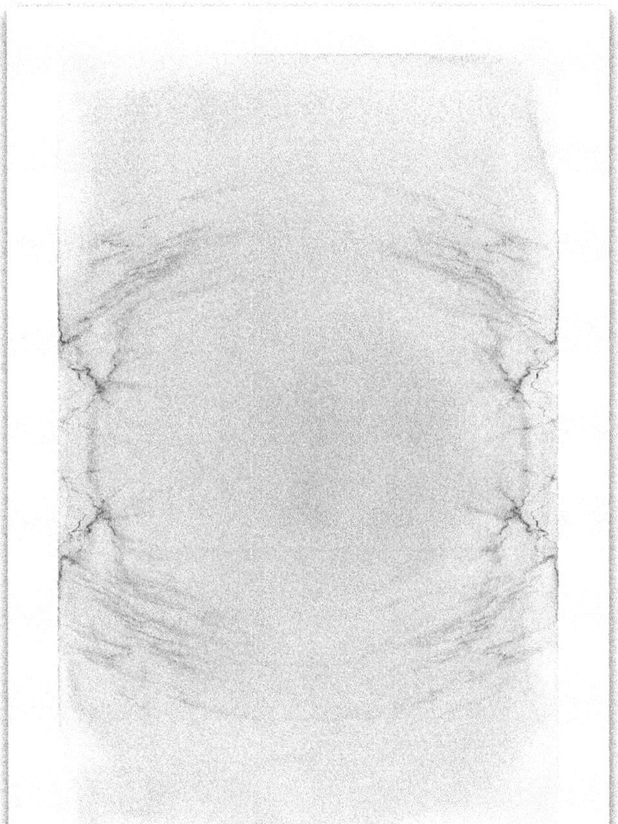

Something passes that feels full of feeling.

But it doesn't carry the person I want it to be.

Like warmth without a body,

or a trace without a source.

Sometimes the disturbance fades on its own.

Not defeated—just loosening, thinning, dispersing.

The absence that follows is plain,

almost awkwardly ordinary.

An attachment forms around a thought.

It behaves as if it wants more of me—

clingy, reactive, insistent.

I can feel the loop without claiming what it is.

A small glow rises—wanting credit.

It offers a story: I am someone now.

The story thickens quickly,

and I feel how it narrows me.

The dream-world responds slightly.

Not like command—more like pressure on soft material.

It makes me cautious,

because response can be mistaken for permission.

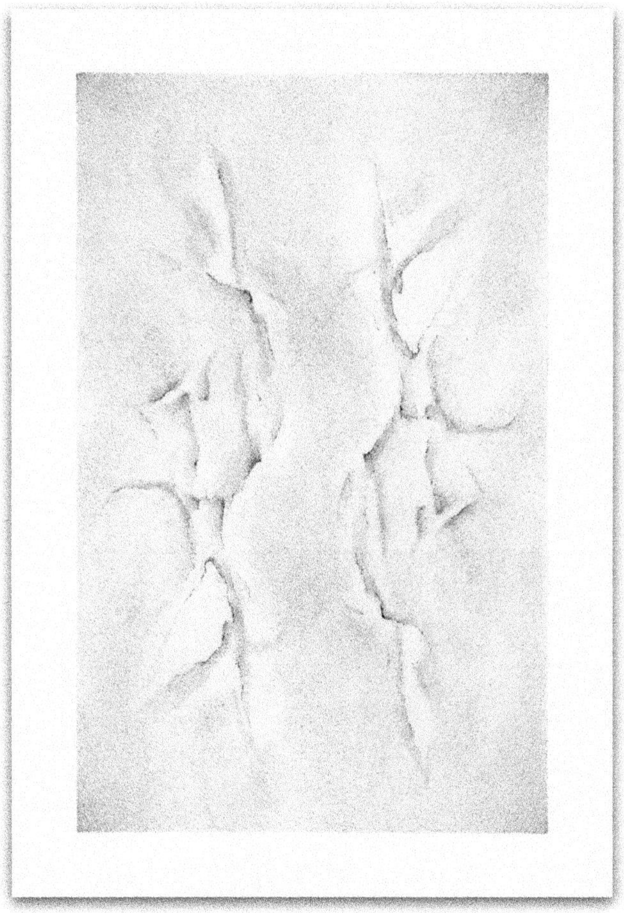

Reality sometimes feels like it stutters.

Devices, timing, coincidence—

not as proof of anything,

just as a thin sense of instability at the surface.

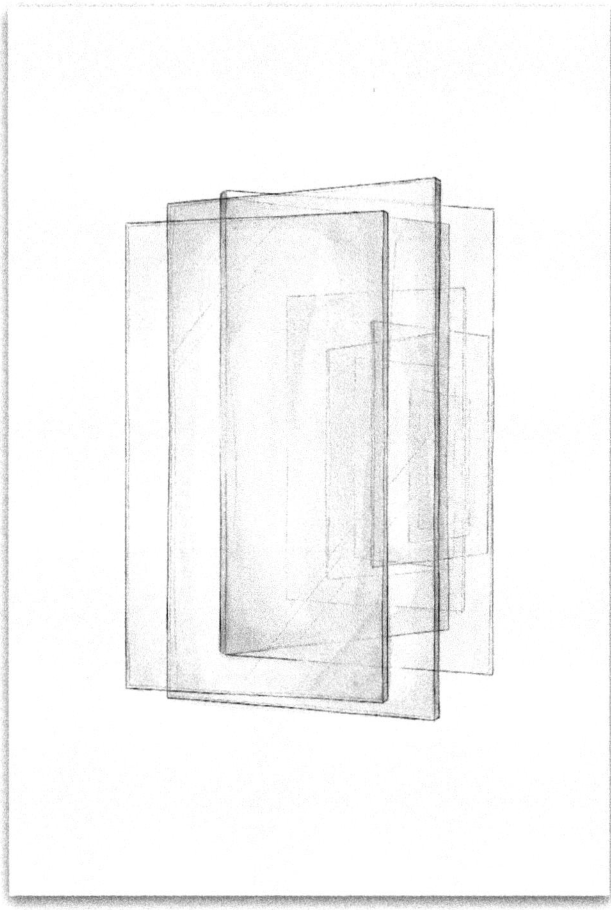

Images arrive too loudly.

Meaning sticks where I don't want it.

The room feels invaded by interpretation,

even when nothing "happens."

A wave of connection comes.

Soft, human, uncontained—

so wide it becomes almost unbearable.

I don't make it a truth.

I just register the size of it.

Chapter 9

I feel close to something simple,

and the closeness makes me nervous.

It's like standing in front of a thin layer I can almost describe

—and noticing that description can thicken it.

An image comes: a field that could hold anything.

Not as a fact—more as a way the mind tries to cope with the amount.

Seeds without labels. Opposites without arguments.

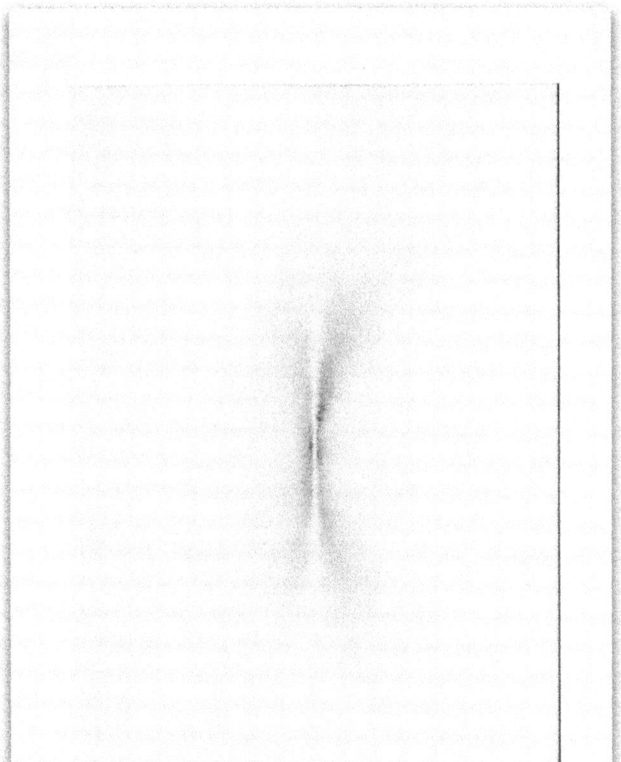

The mind keeps trying to pick a side: full or empty.

But the experience refuses to choose.

It sits there, quietly, with both weights in its hands.

I notice the outline more than the thing.

A missing space becomes strangely active—

as if absence has a texture the mind keeps touching.

Space starts to feel like the main character.

Not mystical—just persistent.

Between every object: the same clear interval, asking nothing.

Too much comes at once.

And somewhere—unseen—something decides what counts as "a thing."

I don't see the switchboard. I only feel the click after.

Order feels clean.

Then it feels airless.

A perfect grid can become a quiet cage without anyone noticing.

Time doesn't shatter.

It loosens, like a straight line remembering it could curve.

I can't prove it. I only register the softness at the edges.

I picture the mind cutting shapes out of the world.

And I start noticing the offcuts.

Not as entities—just leftovers: the negative space that remains when naming is done.

Sometimes I'm absorbed in doing something simple.

And the dividing lines—before/after,

me/that—thin for a while.

When I look for it, it's already gone.

An image of an archive appears—too large to enter.

It doesn't feel like knowledge.

It feels like weight: the idea of everything at once.

I feel close to something simple again.

But every time I try to hold it,

it turns into another object in my hand.

So I let it stay unheld, and I keep walking.

Chapter 10

I look back and can't quite believe the distance.

It isn't victory. It's fatigue with a kind of honesty in it.

The miles are simply there, behind me.

Ordinary conversation lands like weight.

The world looks intact, but my body reacts as if I've dropped too quickly.

Nothing is wrong "out there," and still something in me jolts.

Some moments glow for no reason.

I don't announce them.

The glow doesn't need witnesses to be real to me.

I recognise the shape of mourning.

I've lost a self before.

This time it's a different costume, and the sadness is strangely familiar.

I can't find words for what I've carried.

Even my best sentence feels like a poor photocopy.

The original stays inside, intact and unsayable.

There is a centre I keep returning to.

Not as a practice, not as a claim—

more like a familiar place the mind falls quiet around.

Something that felt close is quieter now.

I reach for it and touch only absence.

The absence is plain—almost tender—yet it stings.

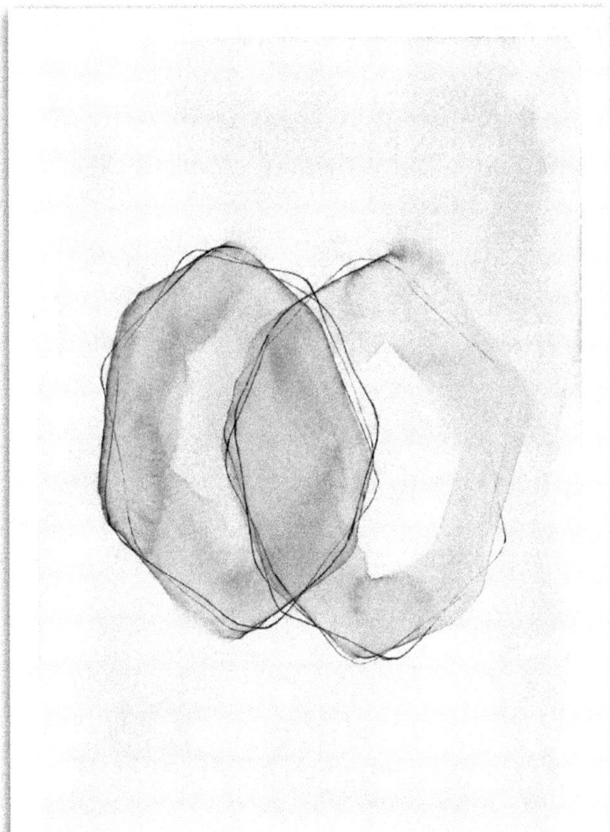

The sadness arrives without a story.

It hurts, but it feels clean.

The edges of it are strangely bright, as if tenderness has its own light.

I notice the masks people speak through.

I don't mean it as blame.

I just don't know how to answer without putting one on too.

Judgement won't hold its shape.

It slides off, leaving a quiet softness behind.

The softness is heavy, because the suffering stream seems endless.

Sometimes the world turns gold without warning.

Not a message—just a shift in how everything is received.

It passes, and the kettle still needs boiling.

Things fall off me.

Old fears, old hooks, old insistences.

I don't do it. I only notice the lightness where they were.

I make something small: sound, colour, shape.

I let it speak without my mouth.

No claim, no lesson—just a trace that feels true.

I step back into the street.

Nothing announces me, and that's the point.

The strange continues quietly underneath, while life stays ordinary above.

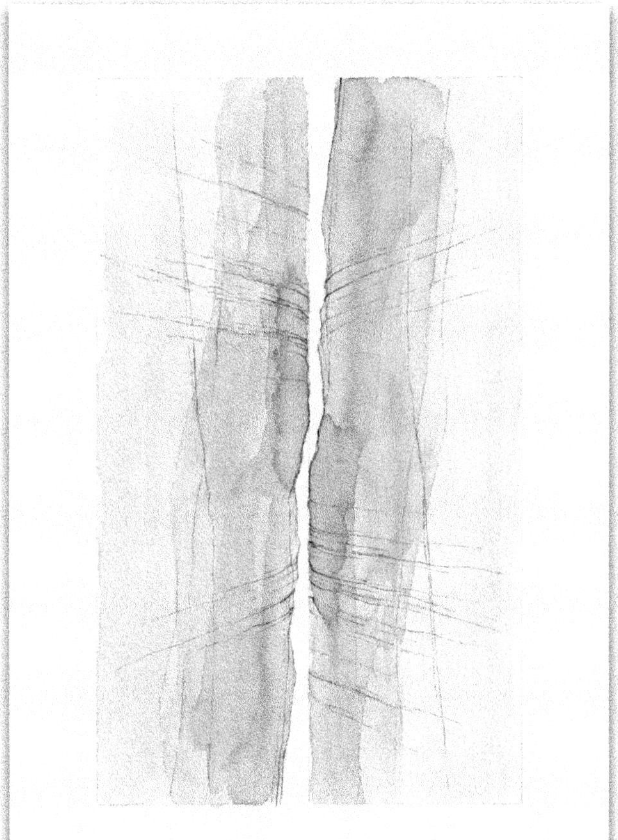

Chapter 11

I return to the words like stones I can step on.

They don't explain me.

They steady me.

Even the map feels half-erased, and still it helps.

Things move through me: mood, thought, sensation.

And something notices without moving.

I can't point to it without turning it into an object.

Every word I reach for becomes a thing.

The moment I name it, it slips behind the name.

I'm left holding the label, and the air where it was.

I feel myself rising through ideas.

And at the same time I doubt there was ever a staircase.

The doubt doesn't cancel the feeling; it just softens it.

One side of me is movement.

Another is stillness.

When I try to separate them, I lose both.

So I hold the strain as it is.

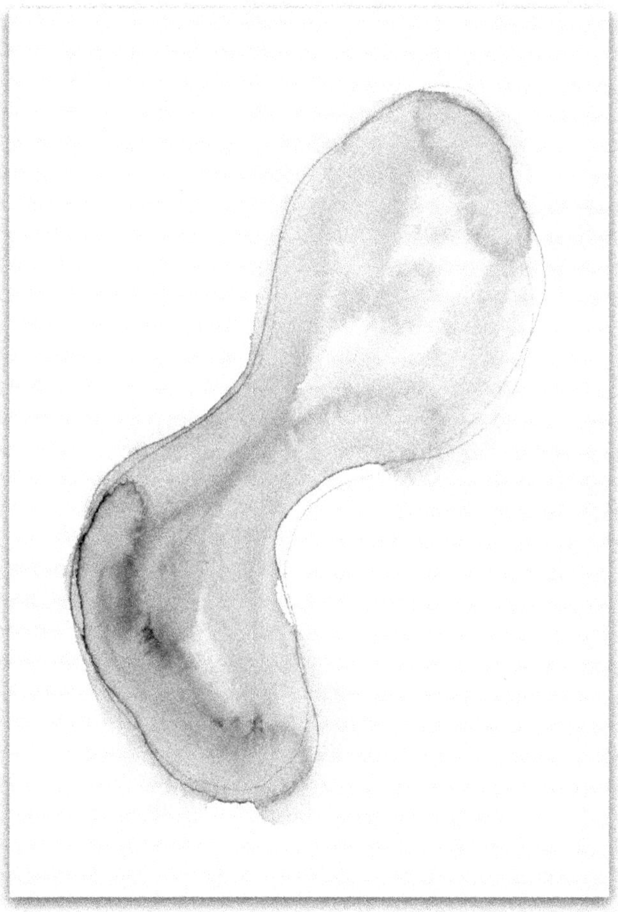

I watch the mind sorting.

Meaningful / meaningless. Good / bad. Mine / not mine.

The sorting happens like a reflex, before I agree with it.

The dark carries a bright seed.

The bright carries a dark seed.

My conclusions start to wobble, not from confusion—

from seeing how each side contains the other.

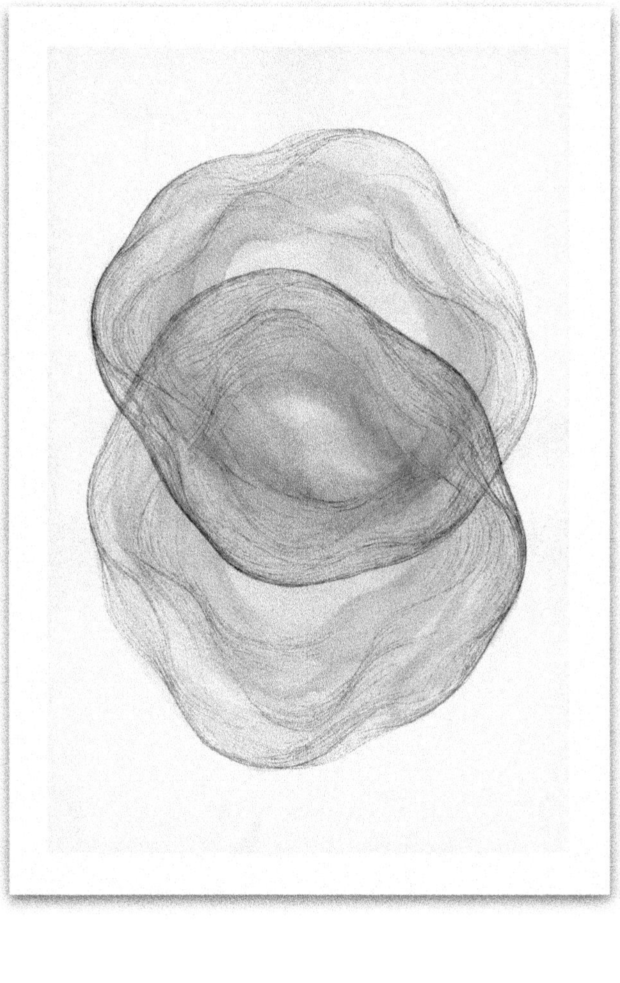

Something draws near without arriving.

It's close enough to soothe me, close enough to unsettle me.

The quiet tightens, and I don't know what it means.

An old story rises as an image.
Fruit. A split. The moment the world becomes
"this versus that."
I don't take it as proof—only as how
the mind remembers division.

The mind gathers at the doorway.

It wants a sign. It wants a story.

The doorway stays plain, and the wanting itself becomes visible.

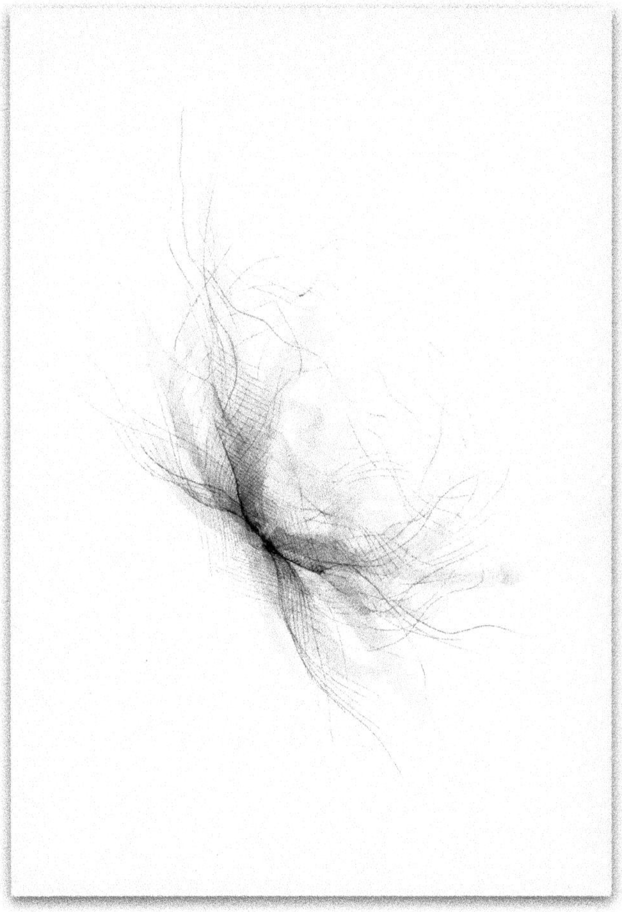

If it happens, it won't feel like winning.

It will feel like the question dissolving mid-sentence—

like the frame quietly forgetting to hold itself.

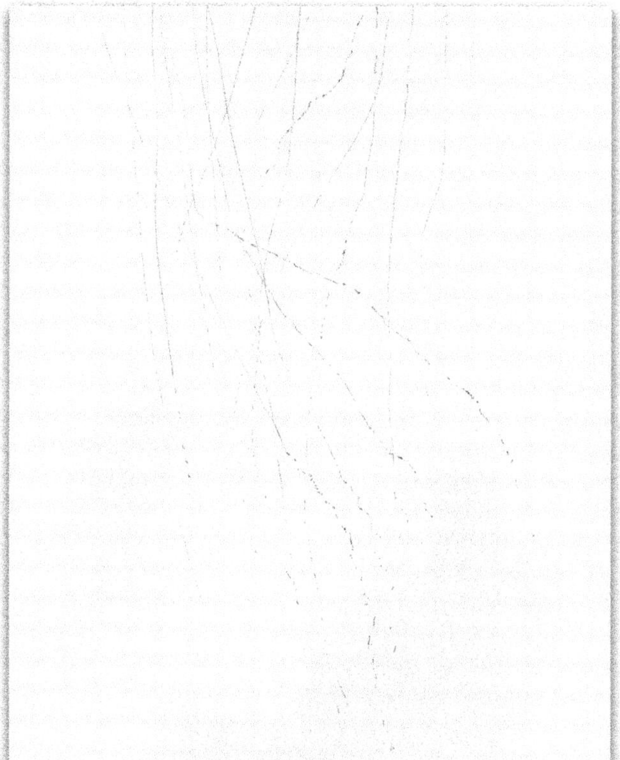

After the conceptual storm, something quieter remains.

I can't say what I understood.

But the way I look feels slightly altered—subtle, persistent, unfinished.

Chapter 12

I arrive and immediately feel how plain it is.

The mind expects fireworks.

It meets a quiet fact, and the quiet holds.

"I" feels like a marker more than a story.

Events pass through a centre that doesn't announce itself.

The centre is ordinary, and that ordinariness is the point.

For a moment, everything reflects everything.

Faces inside faces, light inside light—

dazzling, and strangely impersonal.

It feels like stepping with no ground.

Not falling—just ungripped.

The lightness has risk in it, and also relief.

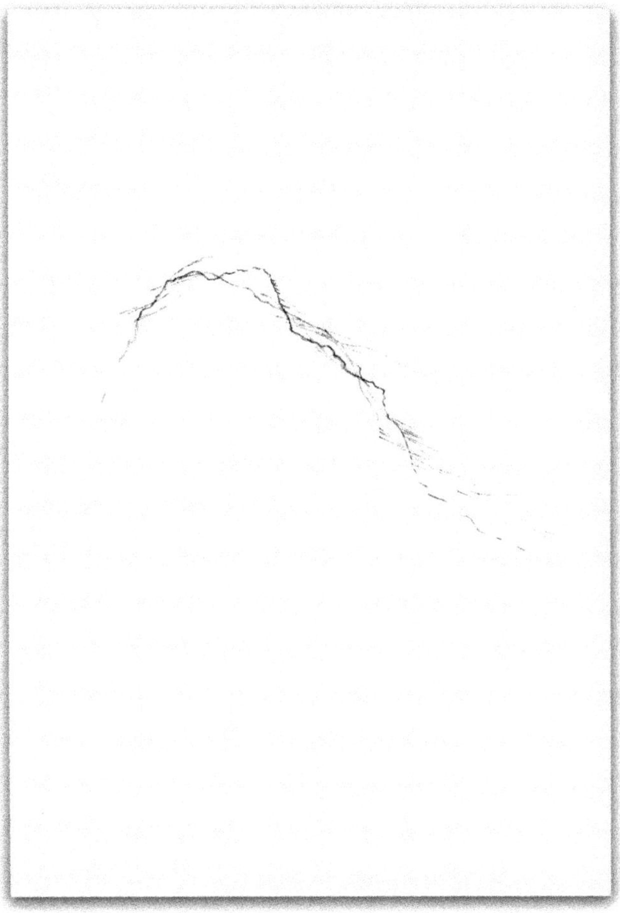

Purpose loosens.

Nothing rushes in to replace it.

The space left behind is clear, almost austere.

Everything glows for a while.

It doesn't feel like a revelation.

It feels like noticing what was already here.

Sorrow rises for others.

It doesn't harden into despair.

It stays tender, bright at the edges, and wordless.

Something finishes.

Something opens.

The mind can't tell if it's loss or release, so it stops trying.

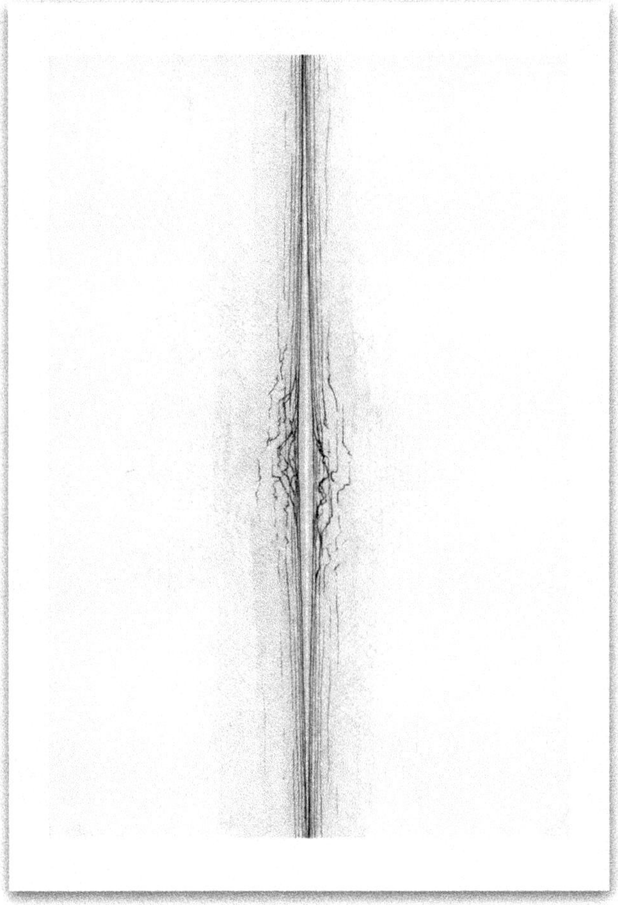

The boundary between "me" and "you" thins.

Not into certainty—into closeness.

It feels like one gaze held gently.

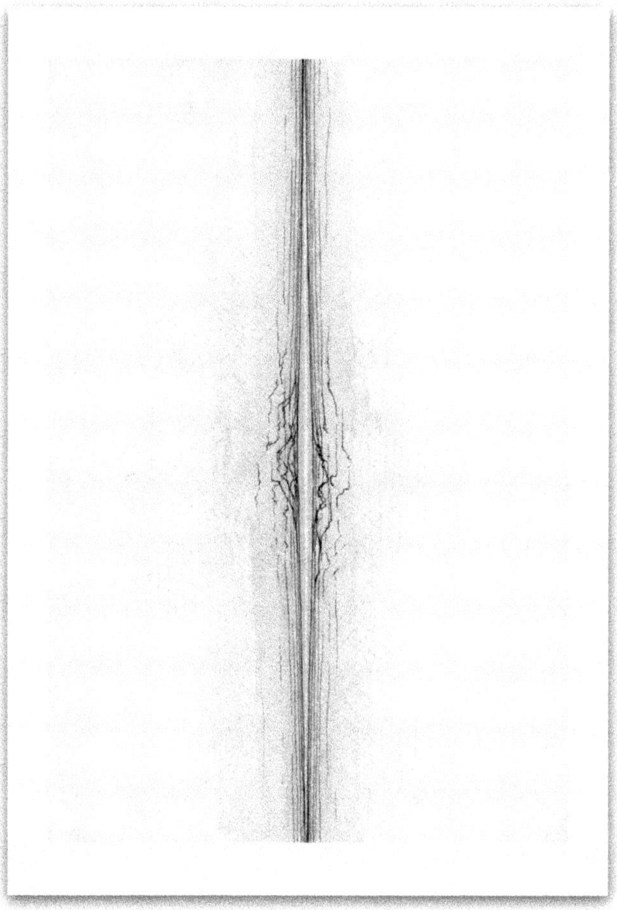

The boundary between "me" and "you" thins.

Not into certainty—into closeness.

It feels like one gaze held gently.

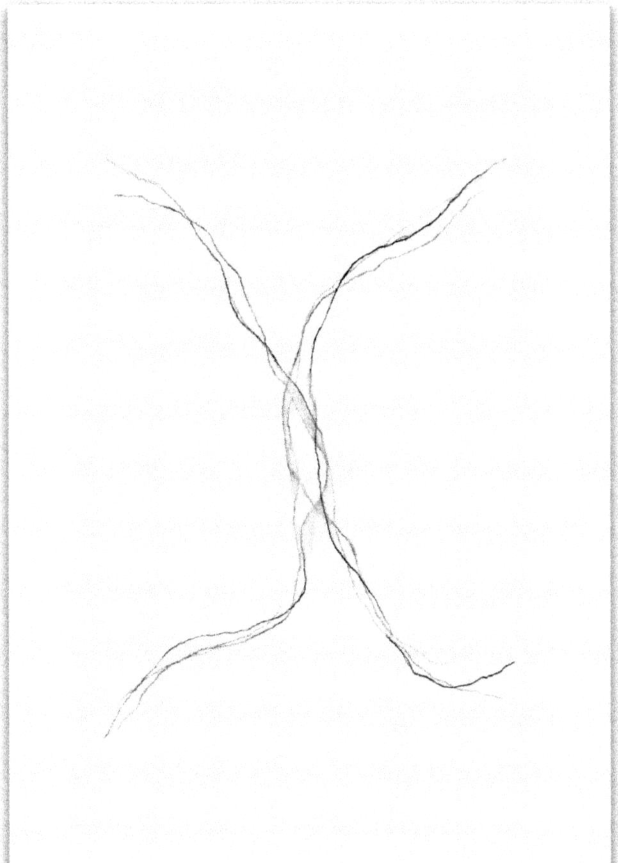

I sense a centre that isn't a point.

An expanse that isn't distance.

The mind can't model it, and the sensing remains.

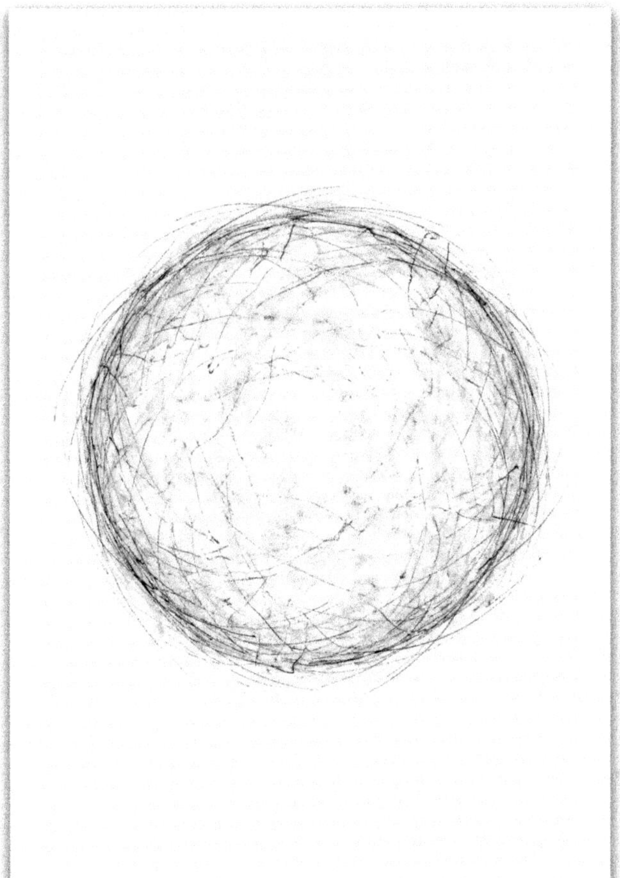

A presence feels steady and unhurried.

It doesn't pull.

It simply remains, like a light left on.

I look around one last time.

Not to conclude—just to see.

Then I leave the seeing where it is, and let the journey continue.

www.ingramcontent.com/pod-product-compliance
Lightning Source LLC
LaVergne TN
LVHW050927210926
848482LV00013B/556

* 9 7 8 1 9 1 8 5 3 2 0 0 5 *